God's Little Instruction Book
FOR THE
CLASS OF 2002

Honor Books

Tulsa, Oklahoma

God's Little Instruction Book for the Class of 2002
ISBN 1-56292-576-8
45-253-00238
Copyright © 2002 by Honor Books
P.O. Box 55388
Tulsa, Oklahoma 74155

INTRODUCTION

Congratulations! As a member of the Class of 2002, you have the privilege and responsibility of being part of the most important group of people on earth—those who will be setting the pace, establishing the values, and initiating the changes for a world that suddenly finds itself face to face with the future.

Like every generation that has come before, you will encounter enormous challenges as well as amazing opportunities. And you are bound to find that you will be confronted with difficult questions and complex issues for which there are no precedents. You will truly be going where no one has gone before—except God! How will you find the answers you need?

In *God's Little Instruction Book for the Class of 2002,* we at Honor Books offer you God's timeless wisdom taken from the one book that will never be obsolete—the Bible. We hope the truths presented in these pages will serve as cherished resources for you as you launch out into the depths of human possibility and potential.

THE BEST THING ABOUT THE FUTURE IS THAT IT COMES ONLY ONE DAY AT A TIME.

"Don't be anxious about tomorrow. God will take care of your tomorrow too. Live one day at a time."

Matthew 6:34 TLB

NOBODY BELIEVED DEEPLY ENOUGH IN SOCRATES TO DIE FOR HIS TEACHING. BUT FOR CHRIST, EVEN UNEDUCATED MEN HAVE MADE LIGHT OF FEAR AND DEATH.

If we live, we live to the Lord; and if we die, we die to the Lord. So, whether we live or die, we belong to the Lord.

Romans 14:8

THE JOURNEY OF A THOUSAND MILES BEGINS WITH ONE STEP.

God did not give us a spirit of timidity, but
a spirit of power, of love and of self-discipline.

2 Timothy 1:7

CLASS OF 2002

God's Little Instruction Book

YOU MAY LAUGH OUT LOUD IN THE FUTURE AT SOMETHING YOU'RE EATING YOUR HEART OUT OVER TODAY.

Our light affliction, which is but for a moment, worketh for us a far more exceeding and eternal weight of glory.

2 Corinthians 4:17 KJV

CLASS OF 2002

GOD IS THE GOD OF PROMISE.
HE KEEPS HIS WORD, EVEN
WHEN THAT SEEMS IMPOSSIBLE;
EVEN WHEN THE CIRCUMSTANCES
SEEM TO POINT TO THE OPPOSITE.

What I have said, that will I bring about;
what I have planned, that will I do.

Isaiah 46:11

8

PURE AND SIMPLE, FAITH NOT LIVED EVERY DAY IS NOT FAITH; IT IS FACADE.

If you do not stand firm in your faith, you will not stand at all.

Isaiah 7:9

THINGS AVERAGE OUT: IF YOU THINK TOO MUCH OF YOURSELF, OTHER PEOPLE WON'T.

When pride comes, then comes disgrace,
but with humility comes wisdom.

Proverbs 11:2

10

FEAR AND WORRY ARE INTEREST PAID IN ADVANCE ON SOMETHING YOU MAY NEVER OWN.

"Do not worry about your life, what you will eat or drink; or about your body, what you will wear."

Matthew 6:25

CLASS OF 2002

NO SIN IS SMALL.

I am troubled by my sin.

Psalm 38:18

CLASS OF
2002

GUTS: GRACE
UNDER PRESSURE.

We have this hope as an anchor for the soul, firm and secure.

Hebrews 6:19

13

ALWAYS DO RIGHT. THIS WILL GRATIFY SOME PEOPLE, AND ASTONISH THE REST.

I want you to stress these things, so that those who have trusted in God may be careful to devote themselves to doing what is good. These things are excellent and profitable for everyone.

Titus 3:8

14

WE ARE ALL FACED WITH A SERIES OF GREAT OPPORTUNITIES BRILLIANTLY DISGUISED AS IMPOSSIBLE SITUATIONS.

Fight the good fight of the faith. Take hold of the eternal life to which you were called when you made your good confession in the presence of many witnesses.

1 Timothy 6:12

15

SMART IS BELIEVING HALF OF WHAT YOU HEAR; BRILLIANT IS KNOWING WHICH HALF TO BELIEVE.

Wisdom and truth will enter the very center of your being, filling your life with joy.

Proverbs 2:10 TLB

CLASS OF 2002

NOTHING SETS A PERSON SO MUCH OUT OF THE DEVIL'S REACH AS HUMILITY.

He guides the humble in what is right and teaches them his way.

Psalm 25:9

17

CLASS OF 2002

NEVER, FOR FEAR OF FEEBLE MAN, RESTRAIN YOUR WITNESS.

"If anyone publicly acknowledges me as his friend, I will openly acknowledge him as my friend before my father in heaven."

Matthew 10:32 TLB

CLASS OF 2002

TODAY IS THE TOMORROW YOU WORRIED ABOUT YESTERDAY, AND ALL IS WELL.

"Will all your worries add a single moment to your life?"

Matthew 6:27 TLB

19

God's Little Instruction Book

WE NEED TO PAY MORE ATTENTION TO HOW WE TREAT PEOPLE, THAN TO HOW THEY TREAT US.

"You must love others as much as you love yourself."

Mark 12:31 TLB

20

CLASS OF 2002

FIRE IS THE TEST OF GOLD; ADVERSITY, OF STRONG MEN.

*Blessed is the man who perseveres under trial,
because when he has stood the test, he will receive the
crown of life that God has promised to those who love him.*

James 1:12

21

THINGS ARE NOT ALWAYS WHAT THEY SEEM.

The LORD does not look at the things man looks at. Man looks at the outward appearance, but the LORD looks at the heart.

1 Samuel 16:7

CLASS OF 2002

DEATH IS MORE UNIVERSAL THAN LIFE; EVERY MAN DIES; NOT EVERY MAN LIVES.

"I have come that they may have life, and have it to the full."

John 10:10

23

WISE MEN ARE NOT ALWAYS SILENT, BUT THEY KNOW WHEN TO BE.

It is not good to have zeal without knowledge,
nor to be hasty and miss the way.

Proverbs 19:2

CLASS OF
2002

THE ONLY THING WE HAVE TO FEAR IS FEAR ITSELF.

God is our refuge and strength, an ever-present help in trouble. Therefore we will not fear.

Psalms 46:1-2

25

CLASS OF 2002

THE ANSWER IS ALWAYS IN GOD.

*"Seek first his kingdom and his righteousness,
and all these things will be given to you as well."*

Matthew 6:33

CLASS OF
2002

WHEN ONE DOOR CLOSES, ANOTHER DOOR OPENS.

Let your eyes look straight ahead, fix your gaze directly before you.

Proverbs 4:25

27

THE TEST OF COURAGE COMES WHEN WE ARE IN THE MINORITY; THE TEST OF TOLERANCE WHEN WE ARE IN THE MAJORITY.

Be on your guard; stand firm in the faith;
be men of courage; be strong. Do everything in love.

1 Corinthians 16:13-14

TO HAVE FAITH IS TO BELIEVE THE TASK AHEAD OF US IS NEVER AS GREAT AS THE POWER BEHIND US.

Now to him who is able to do immeasurably more than all we ask or imagine, according to his power that is at work within us.

Ephesians 3:20

EVERY OAK TREE STARTED OUT AS A COUPLE OF NUTS WHO STOOD THEIR GROUND.

My dear brothers, stand firm. Let nothing move you.
Always give yourselves fully to the work of the Lord,
because you know that your labor in the Lord is not in vain.

1 Corinthians 15:58

God's Little Instruction Book

THERE CAN BE NO SUCH THING
AS A NECESSARY EVIL. FOR IF
A THING IS REALLY NECESSARY,
IT CANNOT BE AN EVIL AND IF
IT IS AN EVIL, IT IS NOT NECESSARY.

*This is what the LORD says:"Stand at the crossroads and look;
ask for the ancient paths, ask where the good way is,
and walk in it, and you will find rest for your souls."*

Jeremiah 6:16

31

CLASS OF
2002

YOU MUST DO THE THINGS YOU THINK YOU CAN NOT DO.

"With man this is impossible, but with God all things are possible."

Matthew 19:26

32

CLASS OF 2002

I TRY TO AVOID LOOKING FORWARD OR BACKWARD, AND TRY TO KEEP LOOKING UPWARD.

I have set the LORD always before me.
Because he is at my right hand, I will not be shaken.

Psalm 16:8

33

COURAGE IS FEAR THAT HAS SAID ITS PRAYERS.

"I have told you these things, so that in me you may have peace. In this world you will have trouble. But take heart! I have overcome the world."

John 16:33

34

WHEN WE LONG FOR LIFE
WITHOUT DIFFICULTIES, REMIND
US THAT OAKS GROW STRONG IN
CONTRARY WINDS AND DIAMONDS
ARE MADE UNDER PRESSURE.

*Perseverance must finish its work so that you
may be mature and complete, not lacking anything.*

James 1:4

35

TEMPTATIONS AND OCCASIONS PUT NOTHING INTO MAN, BUT MERELY DRAW OUT WHAT WAS IN HIM BEFORE.

"The good man brings good things out of the good stored up in his heart, and the evil man brings evil things out of the evil stored up in his heart."

Luke 6:45

CLASS OF
2002

GOD WILL NOT DEMAND MORE FROM YOU THAN YOU CAN DO. WHATEVER GOD ASKS OF YOU, HE WILL GIVE YOU THE STRENGTH TO DO.

So now, go. I am sending you to Pharaoh to bring my people the Israelites out of Egypt.

Exodus 3:10

37

HAVE COURAGE FOR THE GREAT
SORROWS OF LIFE AND PATIENCE FOR
THE SMALL ONES; AND WHEN YOU
HAVE LABORIOUSLY ACCOMPLISHED
YOUR DAILY TASK, GO TO SLEEP
IN PEACE. GOD IS AWAKE.

He will not let your foot slip—he who watches over you will not slumber.

Psalm 121:3

38

FIVE GREAT ENEMIES TO PEACE: GREED, AMBITION, ENVY, ANGER, AND PRIDE.

The LORD blesses his people with peace.

Psalm 29:11

39

God's Little Instruction Book

LIFE AFFORDS NO GREATER PLEASURE THAN OVERCOMING OBSTACLES.

I can do everything through him [Christ] who gives me strength.

Philippians 4:13

NOTHING IS WANTED TO HIM WHO POSSESSES GOD.

*Yes, everything else is worthless when compared with
the priceless gain of knowing Christ Jesus my Lord.*

Philippians 3:8 TLB

41

THE TROUBLE WITH OUR TIMES IS THAT THE FUTURE IS NOT WHAT IT USED TO BE.

We fix our eyes not on what is seen, but on what is unseen.
For what is seen is temporary, but what is unseen is eternal.

2 Corinthians 4:18

42

IT IS LATER THAN YOU THINK.

*The night is far spent, the day is at hand: let us therefore cast off
the works of darkness, and let us put on the armour of light.*

Romans 13:12 KJV

43

A SHIP IN HARBOUR IS SAFE, BUT THAT IS NOT WHAT SHIPS ARE BUILT FOR.

"You are the world's light—a city on a hill, glowing in the night for all to see. Don't hide your light!"

Matthew 5:14-15 TLB

44

CLASS OF
2002

God's Little Instruction Book

THERE IS NOTHING PERMANENT EXCEPT CHANGE.

The grass withers and the flowers fall,
but the word of our God stands forever.

Isaiah 40:8

45

WISDOM IS THE COMBINATION OF HONESTY AND KNOWLEDGE APPLIED THROUGH EXPERIENCE.

Teach us to number our days aright,
that we may gain a heart of wisdom.

Psalm 90:12

46

GOD DOES NOT LOVE US BECAUSE WE ARE VALUABLE. WE ARE VALUABLE BECAUSE GOD LOVES US.

The LORD delights in those who fear him,
who put their hope in his unfailing love.

Psalm 147:11

47

God's Little Instruction Book

THE WORLD IS GOVERNED MORE BY APPEARANCE THAN REALITIES.

*These are a shadow of the things that were
to come; the reality, however, is found in Christ.*

Colossians 2:17

48

THE GOAL OF LIFE IS TO FIND OUT GOD'S WILL AND TO DO IT.

Just tell me what to do and I will do it, Lord.
As long as I live I will wholeheartedly obey.

Psalms 119:33-34 TLB

49

LIFE CAN ONLY BE UNDERSTOOD BACKWARDS; BUT IT MUST BE LIVED FORWARDS.

This is what the LORD says—your Redeemer, the Holy One of Israel:
"I am the LORD your God, who teaches you what is best
for you, who directs you in the way you should go."

Isaiah 48:17

50

IT IS BETTER TO HAVE A PERMANENT INCOME THAN TO BE FASCINATING.

Lazy hands make a man poor, but diligent hands bring wealth.

Proverbs 10:4

51

God's Little Instruction Book

MEN ARE NOT AGAINST YOU; THEY ARE MERELY FOR THEMSELVES.

Bear with each other and forgive whatever grievances you may have against one another. Forgive as the Lord forgave you.

Colossians 3:13

52

CLASS OF 2002

LIFE IS A LOT LIKE TENNIS—THE ONE WHO CAN SERVE BEST SELDOM LOSES.

As we have opportunity, let us do good to all people.

Galatians 6:10

53

THINGS DO NOT HAPPEN IN THIS WORLD—THEY ARE BROUGHT ABOUT.

"Heaven and earth will pass away, but my words will never pass away."

Luke 21:33

54

CLASS OF
2002

DON'T ALLOW THE FUTURE TO SCARE YOU.

Whoever trusts in the LORD is kept safe.

Proverbs 29:25

GREAT MEN ARE LITTLE MEN EXPANDED; GREAT LIVES ARE ORDINARY LIVES INTENSIFIED.

Those who have served well gain an excellent standing and great assurance in their faith in Christ Jesus.

1 Timothy 3:13

CLASS OF 2002

THE GREATER PART OF OUR HAPPINESS DEPENDS ON OUR DISPOSITION AND NOT OUR CIRCUMSTANCES.

I know how to live on almost nothing or with everything.
I have learned the secret of contentment in every situation.

Philippians 4:12 TLB

57

A CANDLE LOSES NOTHING BY LIGHTING ANOTHER CANDLE.

*Carry each other's burdens, and in this way
you will fulfill the law of Christ.*

Galatians 6:2

CLASS OF
2002

TAKE TIME TO DELIBERATE; BUT WHEN THE TIME FOR ACTION ARRIVES, STOP THINKING AND GO ON.

Rise up; this matter is in your hands.
We will support you, so take courage and do it.

Ezra 10:4

DO NOT BORROW TROUBLE
BY DREADING TOMORROW.
IT IS THE DARK MENACE OF
THE FUTURE THAT MAKES
COWARDS OF US ALL.

He will command his angels concerning you to guard you in all your ways.

Psalm 91:11

God's Little Instruction Book

WHO LIVES IN FEAR WILL NEVER BE A FREE MAN.

The LORD is with me; I will not be afraid.

Psalm 118:6

61

CLASS OF 2002

WHEN YOU HAVE ACCOMPLISHED YOUR DAILY TASK, GO TO SLEEP IN PEACE; GOD IS AWAKE.

Trust in the LORD forever, for the LORD, the LORD, is the Rock eternal.

Isaiah 26:4

CLASS OF
2002

THINK OF THESE THINGS: WHENCE YOU CAME, WHERE YOU ARE GOING, AND TO WHOM YOU MUST ACCOUNT.

So then every one of us shall give account of himself to God.

Romans 14:12 KJV

63

CLASS OF
2002

WE LIVE IN DEEDS, NOT YEARS;
IN THOUGHTS, NOT BREATHS.
WE SHOULD COUNT TIME BY
HEART-THROBS. HE MOST LIVES
WHO THINKS MOST, FEELS THE
NOBLEST, ACTS THE BEST.

"In him we live and move and have our being." As some
of your own poets have said, "We are his offspring."

Acts 17:28

CLASS OF
2002

TALK IS CHEAP BECAUSE SUPPLY EXCEEDS DEMAND.

He that hath knowledge spareth his words.

Proverbs 17:27 KJV

65

TO SPEAK PAINFUL TRUTH THROUGH LOVING WORDS IS FRIENDSHIP.

Faithful are the wounds of a friend.

Proverbs 27:6 KJV

CLASS OF 2002

God's Little Instruction Book

NO PASSION SO EFFECTUALLY ROBS THE MIND OF ALL ITS POWERS OF ACTING AND REASONING AS FEAR.

You will keep in perfect peace him whose mind is steadfast, because he trusts in you.

Isaiah 26:3

67

God's Little Instruction Book

BLESSED ARE THOSE WHO SEE THE
HAND OF GOD IN THE HAPHAZARD,
INEXPLICABLE, AND SEEMINGLY
SENSELESS CIRCUMSTANCES OF LIFE.

I am with you and will watch over you wherever you go.

Genesis 28:15

68

FROM THE ERRORS OF OTHERS, A WISE MAN CORRECTS HIS OWN.

Those who are wise will shine like the brightness of the heavens.

Daniel 12:3

69

A GREAT DEAL OF TALENT IS LOST IN THIS WORLD FOR WANT OF A LITTLE COURAGE.

The Lord is with me; I will not be afraid. What can man do to me?

Psalm 118:6

70

God's Little Instruction Book

WITHOUT PRAYER, WE RETURN TO OUR OWN ABILITY RATHER THAN TO GOD.

I am glad to boast about how weak I am; I am glad to be a living demonstration of Christ's power, instead of showing off my own power and abilities.

2 Corinthians 12:9 TLB

71

GOD DWELLS IN ETERNITY,
BUT TIME DWELLS IN GOD.
HE HAS ALREADY LIVED ALL
OUR TOMORROWS AS HE HAS
LIVED ALL OUR YESTERDAYS.

"Surely I [God] am with you always, to the very end of the age."

Matthew 28:20

SOME NEVER GET STARTED ON THEIR DESTINY BECAUSE THEY CANNOT HUMBLE THEMSELVES TO LEARN, GROW, AND CHANGE.

Do not think of yourself more highly than you ought.

Romans 12:3

73

A FRIEND IS ONE WHO COMES IN WHEN THE WHOLE WORLD HAS GONE OUT.

If one falls down, his friend can help him up.
But pity the man who falls and has no one to help him up!

Ecclesiastes 4:10

74

DO ALL THE GOOD YOU CAN, TO ALL THE PEOPLE YOU CAN, IN ALL THE WAYS YOU CAN, AS OFTEN AS EVER YOU CAN, AS LONG AS YOU CAN.

Do not forget to do good and to share with others, for with such sacrifices God is pleased.

Hebrews 13:16

75

God's Little Instruction Book

MAKE YOUR LIFE A MISSION—NOT AN INTERMISSION.

Serve wholeheartedly, as if you were serving the Lord, not men.

Ephesians 6:7

CLASS OF 2002

ONE MUST ALWAYS HAVE ONE'S BOOTS ON AND BE READY TO GO.

"You also must be ready, because the Son of Man will come at an hour when you do not expect him."

Luke 12:40

77

God's Little Instruction Book

IF YOU CAN'T CHANGE YOUR CIRCUMSTANCES, CHANGE THE WAY YOU RESPOND TO THEM.

We know that in all things God works for the good of those who love him, who have been called according to his purpose.

Romans 8:28

CLASS OF 2002

IT OFTEN HAPPENS THAT THOSE OF WHOM WE SPEAK LEAST ON EARTH ARE BEST KNOWN IN HEAVEN.

You are a chosen people, a royal priesthood, a holy nation, a people belonging to God, that you may declare the praises of him who called you out of darkness into his wonderful light.

1 Peter 2:9

79

MAKE HASTE SLOWLY.

*If from there you seek the L*ORD *your God, you will find him*
if you look for him with all your heart and with all your soul.

Deuteronomy 4:29

OUT OF DEBT,
OUT OF DANGER.

Give everyone what you owe him....
Let no debt remain outstanding.

Romans 13:7-8

IF GOD MAINTAINS SUN AND PLANETS IN BRIGHT AND ORDERED BEAUTY, HE CAN KEEP US.

If I rise on the wings of the dawn, if I settle on the far side of the sea, even there your hand will guide me, your right hand will hold me fast.

Psalm 139:9-10

82

I AM AN OLD MAN AND HAVE KNOWN A GREAT MANY TROUBLES, BUT MOST OF THEM NEVER HAPPENED.

I will lie down and sleep in peace, for you alone,
O LORD, make me dwell in safety.

Psalm 4:8

HAPPINESS DEPENDS ON WHAT HAPPENS, JOY DOES NOT.

You have made known to me the path of life; you will fill me with joy in your presence, with eternal pleasures at your right hand.

Psalm 16:11

84

God's Little Instruction Book

THE DAY WILL HAPPEN WHETHER OR NOT YOU GET UP.

A little sleep, a little slumber, a little folding of the hands to rest— and poverty will come on you like a bandit.

Proverbs 6:10-11

85

CLASS OF 2002

God's Little Instruction Book

GOD MADE THE WORLD ROUND, SO WE WOULD NEVER BE ABLE TO SEE TOO FAR DOWN THE ROAD.

"For I know the plans I have for you," declares the LORD,
"plans to prosper you and not to harm you, to give you hope and a future."

Jeremiah 29:11

CLASS OF 2002

THE MOST REVOLUTIONARY STATEMENT IN HISTORY IS "LOVE THY ENEMY."

*This is love: not that we loved God, but that he loved us
and sent his Son as an atoning sacrifice for our sins.*

1 John 4:10

87

PEACE IS NOT AN ABSENCE
OF WAR, IT IS A VIRTUE, A STATE
OF MIND, A DISPOSITION
FOR BENEVOLENCE,
CONFIDENCE, JUSTICE.

Seek peace and pursue it.

Psalm 34:14

88

God's Little Instruction Book

THREE THINGS FOR WHICH THANKS ARE DUE: AN INVITATION, A GIFT, AND A WARNING.

Give thanks to the LORD, for he is good; his love endures forever.

1 Chronicles 16:34

89

CLASS OF 2002

WITHIN YOUR HEART
KEEP ONE STILL, SECRET SPOT
WHERE DREAMS MAY GO
AND, SHELTERED SO,
MAY THRIVE AND GROW.

Above all else, guard your heart, for it is the wellspring of life.

Proverbs 4:23

90

GOD'S INVESTMENT IN US IS SO GREAT HE COULD NOT POSSIBLY ABANDON US.

The LORD appeared to us in the past, saying:"I have loved you with an everlasting love; I have drawn you with loving-kindness."

Jeremiah 31:3

91

BLESSED IS THE MAN WHO FINDS OUT WHICH WAY GOD IS MOVING AND THEN GETS GOING IN THE SAME DIRECTION.

Whether you turn to the right or to the left, your ears will hear a voice behind you, saying, "This is the way; walk in it."

Isaiah 30:21

92

CLASS OF 2002

SOMETIMES I THINK I UNDERSTAND EVERYTHING, THEN I REGAIN CONSCIOUSNESS.

Trust in the LORD with all thine heart; and lean not unto thine own understanding. In all thy ways acknowledge him, and he shall direct thy paths.

Proverbs 3:5-6 KJV

93

DEBT IS THE WORST POVERTY.

The borrower is servant to the lender.

Proverbs 22:7

God's Little Instruction Book

OBSTACLES IN THE PATHWAY
OF THE WEAK BECOME
STEPPING-STONES IN THE
PATHWAY OF THE STRONG.

We are being renewed day by day.

2 Corinthians 4:16

95

THE MARK OF A MAN IS HOW HE TREATS A PERSON WHO CAN BE OF NO POSSIBLE USE TO HIM.

In everything you do, put God first, and he will direct you and crown your efforts with success.

Proverbs 3:6 TLB

CLASS OF 2002

FEAR DEFEATS MORE PEOPLE THAN ANY OTHER ONE THING IN THE WORLD.

Perfect love drives out fear.

1 John 4:18

97

A BURDEN SHARED IS A LIGHTER LOAD.

God is our refuge and strength, a very present help in trouble.

Psalm 46:1 KJV

CLASS OF
2002

God's Little Instruction Book

NEVER FEAR SHADOWS. THEY SIMPLY MEAN THERE'S A LIGHT SHINING SOMEWHERE.

Yea, though I walk through the valley of the shadow of death, I will fear no evil: for thou art with me.

Psalm 23:4 KJV

99

CLASS OF 2002

IF YOU BELIEVE EVERYTHING YOU READ, YOU BETTER NOT READ.

Prove all things; hold fast that which is good.

1 Thessalonians 5:21 KJV

CLASS OF 2002

THE CURE FOR FEAR IS FAITH.

I sought the LORD, and he answered me;
he delivered me from all my fears.

Psalm 34:4

101

God's Little Instruction Book

GIVE YOUR PROBLEMS TO GOD; HE WILL BE UP ALL NIGHT ANYWAY.

"Even the very hairs of your head are all numbered.
So don't be afraid; you are worth more than many sparrows."

Matthew 10:30-31

102

God's Little Instruction Book

HOW YOU THINK ABOUT A
PROBLEM IS MORE IMPORTANT
THAN THE PROBLEM ITSELF.
SO ALWAYS THINK POSITIVELY.

Thanks be to God!
He gives us the victory through our Lord Jesus Christ.

I Corinthians 15:57

103

CLASS OF 2002

God's Little Instruction Book

ALL I HAVE SEEN TEACHES ME TO TRUST THE CREATOR FOR ALL I HAVE NOT SEEN.

*I will say of the L*ORD*, "He is my refuge
and my fortress, my God, in whom I trust."*

Psalm 91:2

104

God's Little Instruction Book

ANY DEFINITION OF A SUCCESSFUL LIFE MUST INCLUDE SERVING OTHERS.

"He that is the greatest among you shall be your servant."

Matthew 23:11 KJV

105

CLASS OF 2002

GOD NEVER PUT ANYONE IN A PLACE TOO SMALL TO GROW IN.

Give thanks in all circumstances, for
this is God's will for you in Christ Jesus.

1 Thessalonians 5:18

106

ACT BOLDLY AND UNSEEN FORCES WILL COME TO YOUR AID.

We have the Lord our God to fight our battles for us!

2 Chronicles 32:8 TLB

107

COURAGE IS THE POWER TO LET GO OF THE FAMILIAR.

The LORD is the stronghold of my life—of whom shall I be afraid?

Psalm 27:1

CLASS OF
2002

DO NOT LET WHAT YOU CANNOT DO INTERFERE WITH WHAT YOU CAN DO.

"Everything is possible for him who believes."

Mark 9:23

God's Little Instruction Book

AND WHAT HE GREATLY THOUGHT, HE NOBLY DARED.

I will not fear the tens of thousands drawn up against me on every side.

Psalm 3:6

110

CLASS OF
2002

WHAT WE CALL ADVERSITY, GOD CALLS OPPORTUNITY.

Rise up; this matter is in your hands.
We will support you, so take courage and do it.

Ezra 10:4

111

CLASS OF 2002

IS HE ALONE WHO HAS COURAGE ON HIS RIGHT HAND AND FAITH ON HIS LEFT HAND?

He does not fear bad news, nor live in dread of what may happen. For he is settled in his mind that Jehovah will take care of him.

Psalm 112:7 TLB

IF *A* EQUALS SUCCESS,
THEN THE FORMULA IS
$A = X + Y + Z$. *X* IS WORK,
Y IS PLAY, AND *Z* IS
KEEP YOUR MOUTH SHUT.

Even a fool is thought wise if he keeps silent.

Proverbs 17:28

113

CLASS OF
2002

God's Little Instruction Book

TRUTH, LIKE SURGERY, MAY HURT BUT IT CURES.

Speaking the truth in love, we will in all things grow up into him who is the Head, that is, Christ.

Ephesians 4:15

THE CAPACITY TO CARE GIVES LIFE ITS DEEPEST SIGNIFICANCE.

*Carry each other's burdens, and in this
way you will fulfill the law of Christ.*

Galatians 6:2

115

IF GOD SENDS US ON STONY PATHS, HE WILL PROVIDE US WITH STRONG SHOES.

*Be strong and let us fight bravely for our people and the
cities of our God. The LORD will do what is good in his sight.*

2 Samuel 10:12

116

GOD LOVES EACH OF US AS IF THERE WERE ONLY ONE OF US.

Christ's love compels us, because we are convinced that one died for all.

2 Corinthians 5:14

117

IT IS AMIDST GREAT PERILS THAT WE SEE BRAVE HEARTS.

I will not fear the tens of thousands
drawn up against me on every side.

Psalm 3:6

118

CLASS OF 2002

THE MIND GROWS BY WHAT IT FEEDS ON.

The mind controlled by the Spirit is life and peace.

Romans 8:6

WE ARE MADE STRONG BY THE DIFFICULTIES WE FACE, NOT BY THOSE WE EVADE.

In all these things we are more than conquerors through him who loved us.

Romans 8:37

120

YOUR TALENT IS GOD'S GIFT TO YOU. WHAT YOU DO WITH IT IS YOUR GIFT BACK TO GOD.

Every good and perfect gift is from above,
coming down from the Father of the heavenly lights.

James 1:17

121

God's Little Instruction Book

DON'T COUNT ON YOUR EDUCATION TO MAKE YOU WISE.

He who trusts in himself is a fool, but he who walks in wisdom is kept safe.

Proverbs 28:26

GIVING IS THE SECRET TO A
HEALTHY LIFE. NOT NECESSARILY
MONEY, BUT WHATEVER A MAN
HAS OF ENCOURAGEMENT AND
SYMPATHY AND UNDERSTANDING.

"It is more blessed to give than to receive."

Acts 20:35

123

CALL ON GOD, BUT ROW AWAY FROM THE ROCKS.

Wisdom and good judgment live together, for wisdom knows where to discover knowledge and understanding.

Proverbs 8:12 TLB

CLASS OF 2002

HE BECAME WHAT WE ARE, TO MAKE US WHAT HE IS.

We ... are being transformed into his likeness with ever-increasing glory.

2 Corinthians 3:18

125

FAITHFULNESS
IN LITTLE THINGS
IS A BIG THING.

Great is his faithfulness; his lovingkindness begins afresh each day.

Lamentations 3:23 TLB

CLASS OF
2002

YOU DON'T HAVE TO LIE AWAKE NIGHTS TO SUCCEED—JUST STAY AWAKE DAYS.

Take up your positions; stand firm and see the deliverance the LORD will give you.

2 Chronicles 20:17

127

SUCCESS CONSISTS OF GETTING UP MORE TIMES THAN YOU FALL.

I can do everything through him who gives me strength.

Philippians 4:13

CLASS OF
2002

I AM CONVINCED THAT FAITH SOMETIMES MEANS KNOWING GOD CAN WHETHER OR NOT HE DOES.

If we are thrown into the blazing furnace, the God we serve is able to save us from it. . . . But even if he does not, we want you to know, O king, that we will not serve your gods.

Daniel 3:17-18

129

THE STARS ARE CONSTANTLY SHINING, BUT OFTEN WE DO NOT SEE THEM UNTIL THE DARK HOURS.

My help comes from the LORD, the Maker of heaven and earth.

Psalm 121:2

CLASS OF 2002

IT IS FAR BETTER FOR A MAN TO SEE HIS OWN FAULTS, THAN FOR ANYONE ELSE TO SEE THEM.

Search me, O God, and know my heart; test my thoughts.
Point out anything you find in me that makes you sad.

Psalms 139:23-24 TLB

131

I HAVE DECIDED TO STICK WITH LOVE. HATE IS TOO GREAT A BURDEN TO BEAR.

Do everything in love.

1 Corinthians 16:14

HE WHO LAUGHS, LASTS.

A cheerful heart does good like medicine.

Proverbs 17:22 TLB

133

IF AT FIRST YOU DON'T SUCCEED, YOU ARE RUNNING ABOUT AVERAGE.

Whatever you do, work at it with all your heart, as working for the Lord, not for men.

Colossians 3:23

134

God's Little Instruction Book

LEARN FROM YESTERDAY;
LIVE FOR TODAY;
HOPE FOR TOMORROW.

We have this hope as an anchor for the soul, firm and secure.

Hebrews 6:19

135

THERE IS NO COSMETIC FOR BEAUTY LIKE HAPPINESS.

A happy heart makes the face cheerful.

Proverbs 15:13

CLASS OF 2002

THERE ARE AT LEAST FOUR THINGS
YOU CAN DO WITH YOUR HANDS.
YOU CAN WRING THEM IN DESPAIR;
FOLD THEM IN IDLENESS;
CLENCH THEM IN ANGER; OR
USE THEM TO HELP SOMEONE.

She opens her arms to the poor and extends her hands to the needy.

Proverbs 31:20

137

BEWARE OF THE HALF TRUTH. YOU MAY HAVE GOTTEN HOLD OF THE WRONG HALF.

Give your servant a discerning heart.

1 Kings 3:9

HE WHO ACCEPTS EVIL, WITHOUT PROTESTING IT, IS REALLY COOPERATING WITH IT.

I will have nothing to do with evil.

Psalm 101:4

139

God's Little Instruction Book

NEVER BE AFRAID TO TRUST AN UNKNOWN FUTURE TO A KNOWN GOD.

I will turn the darkness into light before them and make the rough places smooth.

Isaiah 42:16

140

CLASS OF 2002

THE DIFFERENCE BETWEEN STUMBLING BLOCKS AND STEPPING STONES IS THE WAY A MAN USES THEM.

You need to persevere so that when you have done the will of God, you will receive what he has promised.

Hebrews 10:36

141

WHERE FEAR IS PRESENT, WISDOM CANNOT BE.

The LORD is my light and my salvation—whom shall I fear?

Psalm 27:1

142

TO SEE A WORLD IN A GRAIN OF SAND
AND A HEAVEN IN A WILD FLOWER,
HOLD INFINITY IN THE
PALM OF YOUR HAND
AND ETERNITY IN AN HOUR.

[God] has not left himself without testimony: He has shown kindness
by giving you rain from heaven and crops in their season.

Acts 14:17

143

WHEN I DESPAIR, I REMEMBER THAT ALL THROUGH HISTORY, THE WAY OF TRUTH AND LOVE HAS ALWAYS WON.

The Lord knows how to rescue godly men from trials.

2 Peter 2:9

NO PAIN, NO GAIN.

Consider it pure joy, my brothers, whenever you face trials of many kinds, because you know that the testing of your faith develops perseverance.

James 1:2-3

145

BE WHAT YOU WISH OTHERS TO BECOME.

In everything set them an example by doing what is good.

Titus 2:7

146

CLASS OF 2002

God's Little Instruction Book

BEFORE GOD CREATED THE UNIVERSE, HE ALREADY HAD YOU IN MIND.

The heavens declare the glory of God;
the skies proclaim the work of his hands.

Psalm 19:1

147

CLASS OF 2002

LIFE IS WHAT HAPPENS TO US WHILE WE ARE MAKING OTHER PLANS.

You have made known to me the path of life;
you will fill me with joy in your presence.

Psalm 16:11

148

CLASS OF
2002

God's Little Instruction Book

EVERY ACTION OF OUR
LIVES TOUCHES ON
SOME CHORD THAT WILL
VIBRATE IN ETERNITY.

*"In the same way, let your light shine before men, that they
may see your good deeds and praise your Father in heaven."*

Matthew 5:16

149

FAITH IS NOT MERELY YOU HOLDING ON TO GOD—IT IS GOD HOLDING ON TO YOU.

We live by faith, not by sight.

2 Corinthians 5:7

150

DOUBT IS NOT THE OPPOSITE OF FAITH; IT IS ONE ELEMENT OF FAITH.

"If you have faith as small as a mustard seed, you can say to this mountain, 'Move ... and it will move.'"

Matthew 17:20

151

WHAT GOD DOES, HE DOES WELL.

*I praise you because I am fearfully and
wonderfully made; your works are wonderful.*

Psalm 139:14

152

YOU CAN PREACH A BETTER SERMON WITH YOUR LIFE THAN WITH YOUR LIPS.

*"Even I, the Messiah, am not here to be served,
but to help others, and to give my life as a ransom for many."*

Mark 10:45 TLB

RARE AS IS TRUE LOVE, TRUE FRIENDSHIP IS STILL RARER.

"I have called you friends, for everything that
I learned from my Father I have made known to you."

John 15:15

154

THERE IS NO RIGHT WAY TO DO THE WRONG THING.

There is a way that seems right to a man, but in the end it leads to death.

Proverbs 14:12

155

God's Little Instruction Book

BELIEVE IN SOMETHING LARGER THAN YOURSELF.

*Now faith is the substance of things
hoped for, the evidence of things not seen.*

Hebrews 11:1 KJV

156

CLASS OF 2002

HONESTY IS THE FIRST CHAPTER OF THE BOOK OF WISDOM.

You deserve honesty from the heart; yes, utter sincerity and truthfulness. Oh, give me this wisdom.

Psalm 51:6 TLB

157

ACKNOWLEDGMENTS

We acknowledge and thank the following people for the quotes used in this book: Abraham Lincoln (4), Justin Martyr (5), Lao-Tse (6), Charles R. Swindoll (7,15), Colin Urquhart (8), Jeremy Taylor (12), Ernest Hemingway (13), Mark Twain (14,83), Jonathan Edwards (17), Charles Spurgeon (18,75), Joyce Meyers (20), Lucius Annaeus Seneca (21), Phaedrus (22), A. Sachs (23), Franklin Delano Roosevelt (25), Olivia Leigh (26), Alexander Graham Bell (27), Ralph Washington Sockman (28), Tiorio (31), Eleanor Rooselvelt (32), Charlotte Bronte (33), Dorothy Bernard (34), Peter Marshall (35), John Owen (36), Erwin W. Lutzer (37,68,91,147), Victor Hugo (38,62), Petrarch (39), St. Teresa of Jesus (41), Paul Valéry (42), William Shedd (44), Heraclitus (45), Denis Waitley (46), Archbishop Fulton J. Sheen (47), Daniel Webster (48), Maria von Trapp (49), Soren Kierkegaard (50), Oscar Wilde (51), Gene Fowler (52), Will Hays (54), Tennessee Williams (55), Wilfred A. Peterson (56), Martha Washington (57), Andrew Jackson (59), Dorothy Dix (60), Horace (61), Benjamin Franklin (63), Philip James Bailey (64), Henry Ward Beecher (66), Edmund Burke (67), Publilius Syrus (69), Sydney Smith (70), Beth Moore (71,129), A. W. Tozer (72), Arnold Glasgow (76), Montaigne (77), Tim Hansel (78), Nicholas Caussin (79), Suetonius (80), F.B. Meyer (82), Oswald Chambers (84), John Ciardi (85), Isak Dinesen (86), Eldridge Cleaver (87), Benedict Spinoza (88), Louise Driscoll (90), Ashleigh Brilliant (93), Thomas Fuller (94), Thomas Carlyle (95), Ralph Waldo Emerson (97,104,124), Ruth E. Renkel (99), Norman Vincent Peale (101,103), President George Bush (105), Henrietta Cornelia Mears (106), Dorothea Brande (107), Mary Bryant (108), John Wooden (109), Homer (110), Charles A. Lindbergh (112), Albert Einstein (113), Han Suyin (114), Pablo Casals (115), Alexander MacLaren (116), Saint Augustine of Hippo (117), Jean François Regnard (118), Josiah Gilbert Holland (119), Leo Buscaglia (121), Steven Pagent (122), John D. Rockefeller Jr. (123), Saint John Chrysostom (126), Oliver Goldsmith (128), Earl Riney (130), Emerson (131), Martin Luther King Jr. (132), Mary Pettiborne (133), Corrie ten Boom (140), Lucius C. Lactantuis (142), William Blake (143), Mahatma Gandhi (144), Thomas La Mance (148), Edwin Hubble Chapin (149), E. Stanley Jones (150), Paul Johannes Oskar Tillich (151), Jean de La Fontaine (152), François Duc de La Rochefoucauld (154), Barbara Bush (156), Thomas Jefferson (157), William Frederick Halsey Jr. (158).

Additional copies of this book and other titles from
Honor Books are available at your local bookstore.

God's Little Instruction Book
God's Little Instruction Book for Mom
God's Little Instruction Book for Dad
God's Little Instruction Book for Graduates
God's Little Instruction Book for Students
God's Little Instruction Book—Special Gift Edition
God's Little Instruction Book for Women—Special Gift Edition
God's Little Instruction Book for Parents
God's Little Instruction Book for Leaders

If you have enjoyed this book, or if it has
impacted your life, we would like to hear from you.
Please contact us at:

Honor Books
Department E
P.O. Box 55388
Tulsa, Oklahoma 74155
Or by e-mail at info@honorbooks.com